Rocky Mountains

By Jan Mader

Consultant
Nanci R. Vargus, Ed.D.
Assistant Professor of Literacy
University of Indianapolis, Indianapolis, Indiana

Children's Press®
A Division of Scholastic Inc.
New York Toronto London Auckland Sydney
Mexico City New Delhi Hong Kong
Danbury, Connecticut

Designer: Herman Adler Design
Photo Researcher: Caroline Anderson
The photo on the cover shows Mount Robson, British Columbia.

Library of Congress Cataloging-in-Publication Data

Mader, Jan.
  Rocky Mountains / by Jan Mader.
      p. cm. – (Rookie read-about geography)
Includes index.
Summary: An introduction to the Rocky Mountains, the largest mountain
chain in North America.
  ISBN 0-516-22759-9 (lib. bdg.)   0-516-26832-5 (pbk.)
  1. Rocky Mountains–Juvenile literature.   2. Rocky Mountains–
Geography–Juvenile literature. [1. Rocky Mountains.] I. Title. II. Series.
  F721.M27 2004
  917.8–dc22   2003016935

CHILDREN'S PRESS, and ROOKIE READ-ABOUT®,
and associated logos are trademarks and or registered trademarks
of Scholastic Library Publishing. SCHOLASTIC and associated logos
are trademarks and or registered trademarks of Scholastic Inc.

1 2 3 4 5 6 7 8 9 10 R 13 12 11 10 09 08 07 06 05 04

Did you know that the beautiful Rocky Mountains are often called the Rockies?

The Rockies form the largest mountain chain in North America.

They go from New Mexico to British Columbia. That is about 2,000 miles!

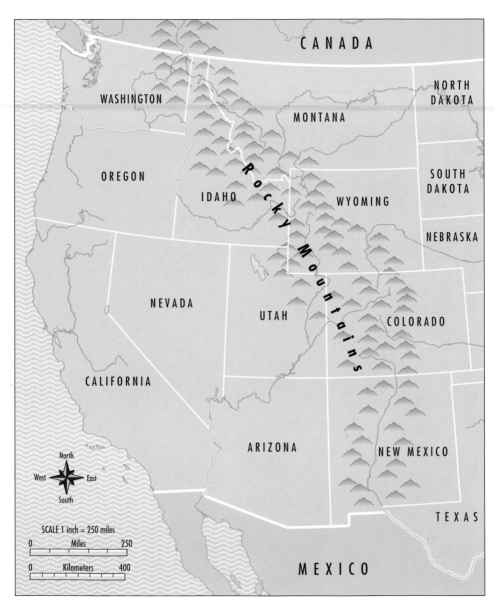

CANADA

WASHINGTON

NORTH
DAKOTA

MONTANA

OREGON

IDAHO

SOUTH
DAKOTA

WYOMING

NEBRASKA

Rocky Mountains

NEVADA

UTAH

COLORADO

CALIFORNIA

ARIZONA

NEW MEXICO

TEXAS

North

West   East

South

MEXICO

SCALE 1 inch = 250 miles

0   Miles   250

0   Kilometers   400

6

The Rocky Mountains are in New Mexico, Colorado, Wyoming, Utah, Idaho, Montana, Washington, and parts of Canada.

Winter in the Rocky Mountains is very cold. Snow can be more than 6 feet deep!

Thousands of glaciers (GLAY-shurs) are found in the Rockies. A glacier is a huge river of ice.

When spring arrives, the snow melts and runs down the mountains. The rivers and streams fill with water.

In the summer, you can see many wildflowers and other plants in the Rocky Mountains.

By early fall, the trees
become dry. They
sometimes catch fire
when hit by lightning.
Then wildfires spread.

The Rocky Mountains
are home to many
different animals.

Bears, mountain lions,
elk, and moose live high
in the mountains.

A bear catching a fish.

Rocky Mountain goats and bighorn sheep live above the timberline.

This area is so high up that trees cannot grow there.

Just below the timberline
is an area called the
krummholz. In German,
this means "crooked wood."

The trees that grow there
are small and twisted.

21

Not many people live in the Rocky Mountains, but a few do.

Some are ranchers who raise cattle and sheep. Others cut down trees for lumber.

Most people who come
to the Rocky Mountains
are visitors.

They visit the beautiful
parks to hike, camp,
and ski.

Some people visit Rocky Mountain National Park and drive on Trail Ridge Road.

It is the highest paved road in the United States.

Other people visit
Yellowstone National Park.
They can see Old Faithful
shoot water and steam
high into the air!

12,005 FEET

Above sea level and higher than Oregon's famed Mount Hood

What would you like to see in the Rocky Mountains?

Words You Know

bighorn sheep

glacier

krummholz

Old Faithful

30

wildfires

wildflowers

Rocky Mountains

Trail Ridge Road

Index

About the Author

Jan Mader has been writing for children for over 15 years. Her natural curiosity and joy of life characterize her work. Jan and her family love to vacation in the mountains. Jan rides horses while her husband and sons go fishing. In fact, Jan can't think of any other place she'd rather be.

Photo Credits

Photographs ©2004: Bob Clemenz Photography: cover, 10; Dembinsky Photo Assoc.: 17 (Claudia Adams), 13, 31 top right (Willard Clay), 9, 30 top right (Ron Goulet), 18, 30 top left (Bill Lea), 22 (Patti McConville), 29 (Jim Nachel), 14, 31 top left (Stan Osolinski), 3 (Dusty Perin); PhotoEdit/Paul Conklin: 28, 30 bottom right; Viesti Collection, Inc./Robert Winslow: 5, 31 bottom left; Visuals Unlimited: 24 (Paul Dix), 26, 31 bottom right (Mark E. Gibson), 21, 30 bottom left (Tom Uhlman).

Map by Bob Italiano